CAROL VORDERMAN'S
14 DAY EASY
DETOX

Carol Vorderman
with Anita

ARROW
DOUGL

First published in Great Britain in 2006 by
Virgin Books Ltd
Thames Wharf Studios, Rainville Road, London W6 9HA

A catalogue record for this book is available from the British Library.

ISBN 0 7535 1120 7

The paper used in this book is a natural, recyclable product made from wood grown in sustainable forests.
The manufacturing process conforms to the regulations of the country of origin.

Designed by seagulls

Printed and bound in Great Britain

CHECK WITH YOUR DOCTOR

Before starting this or any other detox diet programme you should consult your doctor. In particular,
this should be done with regard to any allergies you may have to the foods, drinks, products or other
recommendations contained in this programme. The detox diet may not be suitable for everyone. Pregnant
women should be especially careful and ensure that their doctor advises that the detox diet is suitable for
them. If you are taking medication or have any medical condition, you should check with your doctor first.

While the authors have made every effort to ensure that the information contained in this book is as accurate
as possible, it is advisory only and should not be used as an alternative to seeking specialist medical advice.
The authors and publishers cannot be held responsible for actions that may be taken by a reader as a result
of reliance on the information contained in this book, which are taken entirely at the reader's own risk.

Carol Vorderman
Sole Worldwide Representation
John Miles Organisation
Email: john@johnmiles.org.uk

Carol Vorderman was assisted in the writing of this book by Anita Bean BSc, a nutritionist,
magazine columnist and author of six top-selling books on food and nutrition.

CONTENTS

CHAPTER 1
DETOX IN A NUTSHELL

Are you feeling lethargic, sluggish and a few pounds heavier than you'd like? Do you have a niggling suspicion that you haven't been eating as well as you ought to? Are you unhappy with your weight or worried about your health?

There's no doubt that what you eat makes a huge difference to the way you feel, the amount of energy you have and also your appearance. When you step up your intake of fresh fruit and veggies, nuts and whole grains and cut down on processed meals, sugary snacks and booze, you will feel and look better almost instantly. But when you overload your system with too much fat, sugar and salt, skip meals on a regular basis, and don't take enough exercise, your health and looks will suffer.

Many minor health complaints, such as frequent colds, constipation and lack of energy are the result of poor eating habits, coupled with an inactive or stressful lifestyle. By following this 14-day mini-detox, you will start to reduce or eliminate minor ill-health symptoms, feel more energetic and look more radiant.

What are toxins?

Toxins are substances that are capable of harming your body. These substances may be naturally produced in the body (like carbon dioxide) or they can enter your body from the air you breathe, the food and drink you consume or chemicals absorbed through your skin. In fact, your body is under continual bombardment by toxins from pollutants in the air, cigarette smoke, exhaust fumes, detergents, household chemicals and toxic metals in the environment such as mercury and lead. And then there's the cocktail of pesticide residues and artificial additives in your food that need to be dealt with. Other toxins include alcohol, caffeine, drugs and medications.

What is detoxing?

Detoxing – or, more accurately, detoxifying – refers to the way your body gets rid of potentially harmful chemicals (toxins). It goes on all the time, thanks to the liver, kidneys, skin, digestive system and lymphatic system. In fact, your body is *designed* to cope with toxins. The problem comes when you take in more toxins than your body can efficiently handle or your body's detoxifiers cannot carry out their job quite as well as they should. When your detoxifying systems become overloaded, you may develop symptoms such as bloating, a persistent lack of energy, gradual weight gain and dull skin.

What is a detox diet?

This 14-day mini-detox diet is not about starving yourself, counting calories or obsessively weighing yourself. It's about eating healthily and enjoying tasty meals that help your natural detoxifying systems work properly. It involves limiting the amount of toxins you consume – artificial additives, caffeine, alcohol, salt and sugar – and eating instead nutrient-packed fresh foods.

How can a detox diet improve your health?

Eating erratically, skipping meals and snacking eventually take their toll on your energy levels and your health. Too much sugar, fat, salt or alcohol eventually overburdens your digestive and elimination systems and increases the chances of fat storage. But simply cutting calories is not the answer. Instead, you need to make simple but lasting changes to the way you eat, choose nutritious foods, and learn to eat in a way that suits your lifestyle. This 14-day mini-detox teaches you how to control your appetite naturally, eat only as much as your body needs and get all the nutrients you need for vibrant health.

Are you ready for a detox diet?

Symptoms like achy joints, vague pains, tiredness and headaches are easy to ignore most of the time. You probably put them down to the stresses of everyday living or simply regard them as a natural part of the ageing process. But they are often early warning signs that your body isn't coping with toxins as well as it ought to.

Any stressful period can result in similar symptoms of toxin build-up particularly when you let good eating, exercise and relaxation habits lapse and don't look after your body as well as you should do. Christmas is, of course, the classic time for overindulging in rich food and alcohol. It's hardly surprising, then, that you end up feeling sluggish and bloated in the New Year. Lack of sleep, stress, anxiety and lack of exercise all take their toll on your body. What's more, if you smoke, take regular medications or drink lots of coffee, your poor body has an even bigger toxic load to deal with.

That's where this 14-day mini-detox diet can help you. It will give your poor assailed digestive system a rest. It will help eliminate the overload on your system and restore your natural energy levels. You will quickly begin to feel healthier and more energetic. If you are overweight, you will drop a few pounds too.

How does the detox diet work?

The aim of this 14-day mini-detox diet is to give your body a break from its usual toxin load by reducing the amount of toxins you take in and helping your body's detoxifying systems (such as the liver, kidneys and skin) eliminate toxins more efficiently.

More specifically, it involves:

- Eating nutrient-rich food that encourages the body's natural detoxification processes
- Going organic wherever possible (but don't worry if you cannot always eat organic produce – eating the right types of food is more important)
- Cutting out addictive toxic substances such as nicotine, caffeine and alcohol
- Cutting down on foods and drinks that add to your potential toxin load – processed sugars, saturated and hydrogenated fats, salty foods, and artificial additives

- Reducing emotional and physical stress in your life
- Adopting healthy habits such as regular exercise, relaxation techniques, better sleep and complementary therapies

What will the 14-day mini-detox do for you?

This 14-day mini-detox diet is designed to restore your energy levels, improve your health and make you look and feel a lot better. It's not about calorie counting, strict dieting or measuring out tiny portions of food. It doesn't even require self-discipline, denial or restraint. It's a healthy way of eating – based on ordinary foods – that fits in with your body's natural appetite and nutritional needs. You'll never feel hungry, you'll eat only the foods you like and you won't even need to spend much time cooking. In a fortnight, you'll be bursting with health and vitality.

CHAPTER 2
THE BENEFITS OF DETOXING

Detoxing will do wonders for the way you look, the way you feel and your ability to cope with stress. Perhaps the prospect of shedding your winter layers and wearing a swimsuit on the beach this summer will be all the motivation you need. Or maybe you just want to feel energetic and full of vigour rather than lethargic and run down. Here are ten good reasons to get started on the 14-day mini-detox diet today:

1. You'll lose excess weight

Cut out the biscuits, takeaways and snacks, and eat instead plenty of whole grains, fruit, vegetables, beans, lentils and nuts, and you'll automatically save a lot of calories. According to the world's largest study on successful weight loss, eating a diet high in fruit and vegetables is a vital part of losing weight and keeping it off. A portion (85–125g/3–4oz) of fruit or vegetables provides around 50 calories, whereas one chocolate bar provides 300 calories and four chocolate biscuits, 336 calories. Fruit and vegetables are low in calories, virtually

What is a safe rate of fat loss?

Experts agree between half and one kilo (1–2lb) per week is a healthy and effective rate of weight loss. It is not physically possible to lose more than one kilo of pure fat per week. You may lose more weight than this in the first few days but this is mostly water and stored carbohydrate (glycogen). After this period, losing more than one kilo per week indicates that you are losing muscle, which, in turn, dramatically lowers your metabolic rate (the number of calories you burn each day).

fat-free and filling. If you satisfy your appetite with fruit, vegetables, pulses and whole grains, you'll be less likely to turn to high-calorie snacks. It's a simple calorie balance equation: eat less than your body needs and you lose weight.

2. Cellulite will diminish

Lose fat and you lose cellulite – and that's great news for the 85 per

What is cellulite?

Cellulite is simply fat. The reason it appears dimpled and puckered is that it lies very close to the skin's surface and is crisscrossed by weak collagen strands. This results in the typical bulging appearance of cellulite on your body. The reason women get it far more than men is due to the female hormone oestrogen, which favours fat storage on the thighs and bottom. So women tend to put weight on in these areas. Even regular exercisers can have cellulite if they eat too many calories. Experts also believe that if you spend several hours a day sitting down, the lymphatic system slows down, which results in poor drainage from the fat cells.

cent of us women who are plagued by it. In fact, it affects 95 per cent of women over 30! A healthy but careful calorie consumption combined with exercise are the only proven ways to beat cellulite. On the 14-day mini-detox diet you'll be well on the way to losing that unsightly cellulite.

3. You'll have more energy

Vitality and health are the ultimate aims of the 14-day mini-detox diet. By focusing on fruit, vegetables, salads, whole grains and pulses – foods that are fresh, have not been processed or overcooked and have not been adulterated with artificial additives – you'll be providing your body with all the nutrients it needs to work efficiently. You'll also be reducing the 'toxin' load on your system so you'll quickly begin to feel healthier and more energetic.

4. You'll get fewer colds

On the 14-day mini-detox diet, minor infections such as colds, sore throats and flu are less likely. Fruit and vegetables are the best ways to get high levels of vitamin C, betacarotene and other antioxidants in your diet and research shows that people with high intakes of these nutrients have fewer sick days than others.

5. You'll get rid of bloating

Swallowing too much air and eating in a rush are the most common causes of bloating. During the 14-day mini-detox diet, it is essential that you learn to take your time and sit down to eat. Chewing thoroughly and eating slowly will help reduce the amount of air swallowed with food. You should also avoid drinking fizzy drinks as they introduce more unwanted air. Try plain water and still juices instead. Bloating is sometimes a reaction to certain foods. Cutting out or reducing common culprits such as yeast, wheat products, bran cereals or vegetables from the brassica family (such as cabbage, Brussels sprouts, broccoli, cauliflower) may help.

6. You'll enjoy better health

Numerous studies have linked a diet rich in fruit and vegetables with a lower risk of illness and disease. According to the American Institute for Cancer Research, eating at least five servings of fruit and vegetables each day could prevent at least twenty per cent of cancer cases. Researchers from King's College, London found that people who eat at least 2 apples a week are up to 32 per cent less likely to develop asthma than people who eat fewer apples. And a University of Surrey study found that people who eat the most fruit and vegetables have stronger bones.

7. You can lower your blood pressure

Eating more fruit and vegetables can lower blood pressure. This is due to the high content of potassium, which helps regulate the body's fluid balance. An Italian study found that 81 per cent of people with high blood pressure who started eating 3 to 6 servings of fruit and vegetables a day reduced their medication by half.

8. Your skin will look smoother

Eating more fruit and vegetables and reducing the toxin load on your body improves the clarity and texture of your skin. Your skin plays a vital role in ridding your body of unwanted substances and waste products (via sweating, skin oils and dead skin cells). According to an Australian study, people with diets high in fresh produce had smoother and less-lined skin than those eating diets high in red meat and sugar.

9. Your hair will shine

The vitamins, minerals and phytonutrients in fruit and vegetables do wonders for your skin, hair and nails. A healthy diet tackles beauty problems from the inside, improving the rate of hair growth, cell renewal and collagen formation.

10. You'll feel calmer

Studies show that people eating diets high in fruit and vegetables found it easier to handle stress than those who did not.

CHAPTER 3
THE DETOX DIET PRINCIPLES

The main focus of the 14-day mini-detox diet is nutrient-packed fresh food. Over the next fortnight, you will say goodbye to processed foods that are full of sugar, fat, artificial additives and salt, and eat instead lots of natural unprocessed foods: fresh fruit, vegetables, salads, whole grains, beans, lentils, nuts, seeds and healthy oils.

This means that you will be getting lots more vitamins, minerals, antioxidants and fibre. These nutrients are vital for keeping your body in peak health, allowing your digestive system to process foods efficiently and your elimination system to carry waste products out of the body. They also support the immune system, increasing your resistance to colds and minor infections.

But as well as following the recipes and food suggestions given later, you should follow these basic principles:

1. Do not weigh yourself

Although you may well shed a few excess pounds on the mini-detox, resist the temptation to weigh yourself for the next fourteen days. That's because the main aim is improved health rather than weight loss. Concentrate instead on how your body feels, how much energy you have, how well you sleep, and how good you feel physically and mentally.

Even if your clothes feel looser and you can finally get into those jeans that you have been storing at the back of your wardrobe for ages, try to avoid jumping on the scales every day! That number on the scales is not important. What matters is how much better you will feel.

2. Do not count calories

Unlike other diets, which are designed for weight loss and little else, the 14-day mini-detox diet does not require you to count calories. In fact, you are not expected to count or calculate anything! This detox diet will teach you how to eat sensibly and put together balanced meals. Eventually you will instinctively know how much to eat and what is right for *your* body. Listen to your body and tune into how your body feels.

3. Never go hungry

On the 14-day mini-detox diet you should never go hungry nor miss meals. This is not a starvation diet. Eat when you are hungry. Sounds too good to be true? Well, it really works, because the foods included in this diet – fruit, vegetables, whole grains, pulses – are filling and satisfying. They are packed with fibre and water. They send a powerful signal to your brain that your appetite has been satisfied, so any desire to keep on eating and eating goes away.

4. Eat food as close to its natural state as possible

Eating fresh food means choosing foods that are rich in vital nutrients. You may need to shop more than once a week because many fresh foods don't keep for more than a few days.

Here are some tips on getting the most nutritionally from your food:

- Aim to fill at least half of your plate with fruit and vegetables.
- Food starts to lose its vitamins once it is exposed to air and light, so store vegetables and soft fruits in a cool, dark place. Cut and prepare fruit and vegetables just before using them.
- Buy British if you have a choice – imported produce is usually harvested under-ripe (before it has developed its full vitamin quota) and will have lost much of its nutritional value during its journey to your supermarket.
- Buy fresh-looking, unblemished, undamaged fruit and vegetables.
- Do not buy fresh produce that is nearing its sell-by date.
- When you cook vegetables, try steaming them over a little boiling water so that they retain most of their vitamins. If you must boil your vegetables, use only a little water (about 1–2cm) and add them to the pan only once the water has come to the boil. Cook them until they are only just tender, not soft and soggy. Some vegetables, such as mangetout, green beans or broccoli, taste better when they are still slightly crunchy.

5. Cut the junk!

During the 14-day mini-detox diet you should aim to cut out heavily processed foods from your diet. Foods such as biscuits, crisps and salty snacks, ready-made puddings and desserts, sweets, fizzy drinks and chocolate bars are practically devoid of vitamins, minerals and fibre. They are also packed with saturated fat, sugar, salt and artificial additives. By cutting the junk, you are reducing the toxic burden on your body.

Unprocessed (or minimally processed) foods provide lots of valuable fibre that helps your digestive system work efficiently. You'll also get more vitamins, minerals and phytonutrients (plant substances that protect against illness and improve your all-round health).

6. Get a drinking habit

Make a habit of drinking regularly. Opt for water and – occasionally – juices instead of coffee, tea and sugary soft drinks. Have a glass of water first thing in the morning then drink regularly during your day. Aim for six to eight glasses (1–1½ litres) daily, more in hot weather or when you exercise. It's better to drink little and often rather than swigging large amounts in one go, which promotes urination and a greater loss of fluid.

Carry a bottle of water with you everywhere: to the office, in the car, out shopping. It'll be a constant reminder to drink. It need not be expensive bottled water. A simple water bottle will do – just refill with tap water.

Watching your urine is the best way to check your body's hydration. Dark-gold-coloured urine is a sure sign that you're low on fluid. Drink plenty of water and aim for light-yellow-coloured urine.

WHAT TO DRINK
Not all of your daily fluid needs to be in the form of water. Count the following towards your daily fluid intake:

- Fresh fruit juice, ideally diluted one part of juice to one or two parts of water
- Home-made juices
- Herbal tea, e.g. peppermint, camomile, fennel
- Fruit tea
- Green tea
- Rooibos tea
- Clear soup

Cutting down on caffeine

One or two cups of coffee or tea a day probably won't do you any harm at all. But if you normally drink more than three cups a day, try substituting caffeine-free drinks for some of these. You may find that you feel better for it and that symptoms of caffeine sensitivity – trembling or shaking, increased fluid losses through urine, restlessness, increased heart and breathing rate – disappear.

If you decide to cut down on caffeine, you must *cut back gradually before you begin* the 14-day mini-detox. Do not cut caffeine out quickly, otherwise you will get withdrawal symptoms such as persistent headaches and irritability.

7. Listen to your body

During the next fourteen days, learn to listen to your body's hunger signals. This may take a bit of practice, as it can be difficult at first to work out whether it's food or drink that your body really needs, or whether you just think you're hungry due to boredom, stress or habit. If you have no idea when you are hungry, then don't eat – it means you aren't hungry. On the other hand, don't wait until you are very hungry or starving before eating. Otherwise you will end up eating the wrong foods or overeating.

Try to gauge how much food your body really needs. Respond to your body and simply eat the amount that is right for you. Over the next fortnight you will become attuned to your body's needs and learn to eat the types and amounts of food that are right for you.

8. Enjoy eating

Eating should be a pleasurable experience, so make time to shop, prepare and savour your food. When you sit down to eat, taste every mouthful and enjoy every bite. Stop eating the moment you stop savouring the food or the moment you are full. It's easier to notice you are full if you pay attention while you are eating. That way, your body sends you a message that it is satisfied. But if you don't concentrate while you eat, your body may be telling you it's full but you may override the feeling of fullness and overeat.

9. Improve your lifestyle

The 14-day mini-detox diet is about giving your body a rest from processed food and alcohol, restoring nutrients and revitalising. It also means putting aside time to reassess, regain control and strengthen your mind, body and soul. These other aspects of your lifestyle go beyond the remit of this book but have a big impact on your energy levels and overall health. A happy and positive state of mind can boost your immunity and wellbeing. Developing a positive mental attitude, greater self-belief, more confidence, and gaining support from your family and friends all improve your chances of success in achieving peak health. The following are vitally important:

- Not smoking
- Taking enough exercise
- Limiting drugs and medications
- Dealing with stress effectively
- Dry skin brushing (see below)

10. Make your skin glow

As well as following the eating plan, it is important to treat your skin well too. Daily brushing with a dry skin (natural bristle) brush or loofah gets rid of dead skin cells and debris, allows your skin to 'breathe' and stimulates your circulation. It will make an enormous difference to your skin's appearance and texture. After two weeks, it will look brighter, clearer and feel much softer. Start at the soles of your feet and work up your legs, front, chest, back, hands and arm. Use firm long strokes directed towards your heart to encourage better blood flow.

CHAPTER 4
THE DETOX FOOD RULES

The 14-day mini-detox diet is not a starvation regime; it's not about counting calories. It's all about eating more and enjoying tasty meals. You will be eating more of the delicious healthy foods that do your body good, boost your energy levels, make your skin glow and help you lose inches. Here's a guide to what you can eat and what you should avoid on the 14-day mini-detox diet.

Fruit and Vegetables

Aim for at least five daily portions. That's the amount the World Health Organisation has estimated we need to protect ourselves from cancer and heart disease and provide the minimum doses of vitamins, minerals and fibre we need to stay healthy. But only one in ten people eat this amount. What's more, experts at the US National Cancer Institute believe that nine servings a day may be even better. Their mantra 'Eating 5 to 9 and Feeling Fine: Fruits and Vegetables Anytime' is supported by studies showing that people who ate five a day had half the risk of certain cancers than those who didn't reach the recommended range. According to the American Dietetic Association you should try to have two to three servings of fruit and then really try to bulk up on the vegetables because they are so low in calories.

WHAT'S A PORTION OF FRUIT?

About the size of a tennis ball, for example:

- 1 medium fruit, e.g. apple, orange, banana, peach
- 2 small fruit, e.g. kiwi fruit, plums, satsumas, apricots
- 1 cupful of berries, e.g. strawberries, raspberries, cherries, grapes
- 1 large slice of large fruit, e.g. melons, mangos, pineapples

WHAT'S A PORTION OF VEGETABLES?

About the size of your hand, for example:

- 1 dessert bowl of salad vegetables, e.g. lettuce, salad leaves
- 2 tablespoons (80g) of cooked vegetables, e.g. broccoli, cauliflower, carrots, green beans, peppers, peas, mangetout

Organic choice

Choosing organic food will go a long way towards reducing your intake of toxins – pesticide residues, antibiotics, nitrates and hormones – but the price of organic food means that it isn't always realistic. If you can't eat organic all the time, just concentrate on organic versions of salads and fruit, especially berries and soft fruit, as these foods are the most heavily sprayed and have the highest pesticide-residue content. For other fruits and vegetables, wash them thoroughly in water or remove the peel.

Grains, Bread and Pasta

Grains are the main sources of complex carbohydrates in the 14-day mini-detox diet. These foods provide energy for daily activities and exercise. They are also rich in fibre, B-vitamins (such as thiamin and niacin), vitamin E and minerals (such as iron). Choose the whole-grain (unrefined) varieties rather than refined 'white' versions, which have been stripped of most of their vitamins, minerals and fibre.

Try to replace wheat with other grains for fourteen days. If you have previously eaten a lot of wheat products – pasta, cereals and bread – you may have developed a mild sensitivity to these foods and become prone to symptoms such as bloating and wind. Swapping wheat for other grains – oats, brown rice, millet, quinoa – or for sweet potatoes or potatoes may help to alleviate your symptoms. After completing the mini-detox, you can try gradually reintroducing wheat products into your diet.

TIPS

- Brown rice makes a delicious base for summer salads or fillings for summer vegetables such as red peppers and aubergines. To save time, try the parboiled variety, which takes only ten minutes to cook.
- Oats are also a good source of B-vitamins, iron, magnesium and zinc. Use in porridge, muesli or fruit crumbles.
- Millet is a good source of magnesium and iron. Eat it boiled (like rice) or as a porridge, or add millet flakes to muesli and fruit crumbles.
- Unlike wheat, rye contains no gluten, so switching breads may reduce symptoms like bloating and wind if you are sensitive to gluten.

- Quinoa (pronounced 'keenwa') looks like a grain but is, in fact, a fruit. It contains more protein than grains and makes a tasty alternative to rice or pasta.

Beans, Lentils and Peas

Beans, lentils and peas (known collectively as pulses) are packed with protein, complex carbohydrates, fibre, B-vitamins, iron, zinc, manganese and magnesium, so they make a healthy alternative to animal proteins. They also provide soluble fibre, which combines with water in the gut to make a gummy substance that slows digestion and absorption of food. This helps regulate blood-glucose levels and makes you feel full for longer. They also help to lower blood cholesterol and prevent heart disease. Chickpeas are particularly valuable because they contain fructo-oligosaccharides, a type of fibre that increases the friendly bacteria of the gut – especially useful if your gut bacteria get upset by travel or stress.

TIPS

- If cooking dried pulses, soak them overnight, drain and cook them in fresh water until they are soft (follow the instructions on the packet). Add a little salt-free vegetable bouillon, if you wish, but do not add salt until they have been cooked.
- For convenience, buy tinned pulses. Drain and rinse if they have been tinned in salted water.
- Help your digestive system adapt to pulses by starting off with only small quantities (one or two tablespoons twice a week), and gradually increasing the amount (up to three or four tablespoons daily) as you get accustomed to them.

- Red kidney beans, chickpeas and flageolet beans are delicious in salads, adding texture as well as vital nutrients.

Nuts and Seeds

Far from being 'fattening', nuts and seeds are nutritional powerhouses. They are full of essential fats, protein, fibre, B-vitamins, iron, zinc and magnesium. Although they provide a lot of calories per 100g, they come mainly from heart-healthy monounsaturated oils – which help to lower blood-cholesterol levels and protect against heart attacks – and the vital omega-3 and omega-6 oils. According to a US study of 21,000 male doctors, those who ate two one-ounce servings of nuts each week were 30 per cent less likely to die from heart disease than those who rarely or never ate nuts.

TIPS

- To achieve the optimal intake of essential fats, you need to eat around a heaped tablespoon of nuts or seeds a day. Eat as snacks, sprinkled on salads or breakfast cereals.
- Buy the unsalted kind without spicy or sugary coatings. Toasting them lightly under a hot grill or in a hot oven for a few minutes brings out their flavour.
- Pumpkin seeds and linseeds (flaxseeds) are particularly rich in the omega-3 oils, which are lacking in most people's diets. Linseeds have a very tough outer husk, which is practically impenetrable by digestive enzymes, so you'll need to grind them in a coffee grinder to benefit from the oils. Add to muesli, yoghurt, shakes and smoothies.
- When buying nuts and seeds, check the use-by date is several

months away to ensure they are as fresh as possible. Store in an airtight container in a dark place, as they can quickly turn rancid if exposed to light and air.

Non-Dairy Produce

Many people find that symptoms such as bloating, wind, nasal congestion or a runny nose improve once they give their system a break from dairy products. However, you may gradually reintroduce these foods after fourteen days.

Instead, use non-dairy equivalents of milk such as rice milk, soya milk, almond milk and oat milk. Soya and almond milk provide protein and most brands are fortified with calcium. Non-dairy milks usually contain healthy oils (e.g. rape seed), which boost their content of healthy unsaturated fats.

Tofu is bean curd made from soya beans. You can buy it from supermarkets and it is a useful way of getting protein and calcium while you are following the 14-day mini-detox. It doesn't have much taste on its own but readily absorbs the flavours of any marinade or dressing.

Healthy Oils

Another way to get essential fats is to use cold-pressed oils. Rapeseed oil, extra-virgin olive oil, linseed (flaxseed) oil, walnut oil and sesame oil are rich in the omega-3 and omega-6 fatty acids, which protect against heart disease.

TIPS

- If oils are your only source of essential fats you need about one level tablespoon a day.
- Use omega-3-rich cold-pressed oils (such as walnut oil and linseed oil) in dressings or stir a spoonful into soups and sauces. Don't fry with these oils, as high temperatures will reduce their nutritional value.
- When buying olive oil, choose extra-virgin olive oil, as it is cold-pressed and contains higher levels of antioxidants than ordinary olive oil. It is rich in monounsaturated oil and omega-6 oils and can be used for stir-frying as well as dressings.
- Try cold-pressed oil blends, containing a mixture of linseed (flaxseed) oil and other oils to give you a good balance of omega-3 and omega-6. Store them in the fridge to stop them from going rancid.

Herbs and Spices

Avoid salt and keep salt in cooking to a minimum while on the 14-day mini-detox. If you must use salt, and where it is suggested in a recipe, use herb salt (available from health stores) or a low-sodium salt (available from supermarkets).

You can enhance the flavour of your food with herbs, such as basil, oregano, mint and parsley, or try lemon juice, lime juice, freshly ground black peppers, chilli, cider and balsamic vinegar. Spices, such as coriander and ginger, are also good for detoxing as they help digestion.

Snacks

If you feel hungry between meals, have a healthy snack. Here are some suggestions on what to eat:

- A bowl of strawberries, raspberries, blueberries or blackberries
- A bunch of grapes
- A peach, nectarine or kiwi fruit
- A couple of plums or apricots
- A large slice of melon or pineapple
- A bowl of fresh fruit salad
- A banana
- Vegetables crudités with hummus or avocado dip
- A small handful of unsalted nuts (plain or toasted)
- A small handful of (unsulphured) dried fruit
- A small handful of seeds (plain or toasted)
- A glass of juice
- A smoothie

What to eat checklist

- Fresh fruit
- Vegetables
- Salad
- Unrefined non-wheat cereals – whole-grain (brown) rice, oats, millet, quinoa, rye, buckwheat
- Non-wheat bread – rye bread, wheat-free, pumpernickel
- Non-wheat pasta – corn, millet or rice pasta
- Non-wheat crispbreads – rye, rice cakes, oatcakes
- Water, herbal or fruit tea, pure fruit juice
- Beans, lentils and peas

- Tofu and Quorn
- Non-dairy milk – soya, rice, oat, almond or sesame milk
- Nuts – almonds, cashews, hazelnuts, Brazils, pecans, peanuts
- Seeds – pumpkin, sunflower, sesame, ground linseeds (flaxseeds)
- Extra-virgin olive oil, rapeseed, walnut, linseed (flaxseed) or sesame oil
- Cold-pressed oil blends containing a mixture of omega-3-rich and omega-6-rich oils
- Fresh herbs

What to avoid checklist

- Coffee, tea and other caffeine drinks (including decaffeinated drinks)
- Dairy products – milk, cheese, yoghurt, cream
- Sugar
- Cakes, biscuits, confectionery
- Meat
- Fish
- Eggs
- Wheat bread, pasta, noodles, crackers
- White rice
- Ready meals
- Salt
- Alcohol
- Artificial food additives
- Fried foods
- Artificial sweeteners
- Hydrogenated fats
- Fizzy drinks
- Squashes and cordials

CHAPTER 5
DETOX NUTRITION GUIDE

Here is a quick guide to the main nutrients your body needs and how you can obtain them on the 14-day mini-detox diet.

Carbohydrates

Carbohydrates are your main source of energy. Your brain, nervous system and heart need a constant supply of carbohydrates. You also need them to fuel your daily activities.

Generally speaking, processed sugary and starchy foods (such as cakes, confectionery, white bread, sweetened breakfast cereals) have a high glycaemic index, which means they produce a fast surge of glucose in your bloodstream. This energy buzz is usually only short-lived as your pancreas pumps out insulin to bring your blood-sugar levels back down. Sometimes it overcompensates and your blood-sugar levels dip too low, resulting in fatigue and hunger.

High-fibre carbohydrate-rich foods such as beans, lentils, oats, fruit and vegetables have a low GI, which means they release their energy

What is fibre?

Fibre helps your digestive system work properly and is also useful for weight control. There are two kinds of fibre – insoluble and soluble. Most plant foods contain both but proportions vary. Good sources of insoluble fibre include whole grains (e.g. brown rice, rye bread, whole-wheat bread) and vegetables. These foods help speed the passage of food through your gut, prevent constipation and bowel problems and make you feel full after eating. Soluble fibre – found in oats, beans, lentils, fruit and vegetables – reduces harmful LDL-cholesterol levels, helps control blood-glucose levels by slowing glucose absorption, reduces hunger and improves appetite control.

slowly. They make you feel satisfied for longer and less inclined to snack on unhealthy foods. Combine them with protein or some healthy fat – e.g. rice with beans or fresh fruit with a handful of nuts – and you'll get longer-lasting energy.

Protein

Protein is made up of building blocks called amino acids, which are used to repair cells and to make enzymes, hormones and antibodies. Eight of these – the 'essential amino acids' – must be provided in your diet, while the remaining twelve can be made by your body. For your body to use food proteins properly, all eight essential amino acids have to be present. Meat, fish, eggs and dairy products are rich sources of essential amino acids but you can get also get them from plant sources such as beans, lentils, soya, Quorn, whole grains, nuts and seeds. They contain smaller amounts than animal sources, so they should be combined together (e.g. Puy lentil and tomato salad with walnuts (see recipe, page 104), or hummus (see recipe, page 65) with bread) to make a full complement of amino acids. The general rule of thumb is to have grains and pulses, nuts and grains, or pulses and nuts together.

Healthy Fats

Scientists have discovered that a moderate intake of healthy fats is associated with lower blood-cholesterol levels, lower heart-disease risk and better long-term weight control. Switch *saturated* (animal) fats and *processed* (hydrogenated) fats for *monounsaturated* fats and *essential* fats (omega-3 and omega-6 fats).

STEER CLEAR OF SATURATED FATS

Animal fats (meat, dairy products, butter) as well as products made with palm oil or palm-kernel oil (a highly saturated fat) have no beneficial role in keeping the body healthy – they raise blood-cholesterol levels and increase the risk of heart disease – so try to keep your intake as low as possible.

BAN TRANS FATS

Trans fats, found in hydrogenated and partially hydrogenated oils, are even more harmful than saturated fats. They increase your levels of LDL ('bad') cholesterol while lowering HDL ('good') cholesterol, pushing up your heart-disease risk.

MONOUNSATURATED FATS ARE FINE IN MODERATION

Most of your fat intake should come from monounsaturated fats – olive oil, nuts, seeds, avocados and rapeseed oil. They help to lower harmful cholesterol levels and can cut your heart-disease and cancer risk.

GO EASY ON POLYUNSATURATED FATS

In moderation, polyunsaturated fats also reduce your heart-disease risk, though less effectively than monounsaturated fats.

BOOST OMEGA-3 FATS

You need only tiny amounts of omega-3 fats to keep you healthy but, as they are found in relatively few foods, many people struggle to meet the minimum requirement of 0.9g a day. For heart-disease prevention, better oxygen delivery to your cells, reduced joint pain and stiffness and healthy skin, include one tablespoon of an omega-3-rich oil daily or a heaped tablespoon of nuts or seeds a day.

EAT OMEGA-6 FATS IN MODERATION

Omega-6 fats – found in sunflower oil, corn oil and most spreads and margarines – are also required for peak health. But most people currently eat too much omega-6 in relation to omega-3, which results in an imbalance of prostaglandins – 'mini' hormones – which are responsible for controlling blood clotting, inflammation and the immune system. By eating more omega-3s, you'll automatically improve the balance of these essential fats.

Vitamins and Minerals

Vitamins support the immune system, help the brain function properly and help convert food into energy. They are important for healthy skin and hair, controlling growth and balancing hormones. Some vitamins – the B-vitamins and vitamin C – must be provided by the diet each day, as they cannot be stored.

Minerals are needed for structural and regulatory functions, including bone strength, haemoglobin manufacture, fluid balance and muscle contraction.

Antioxidants

Antioxidants – which neutralise the effects of free radicals – include vitamins (betacarotene, vitamin C, vitamin E), minerals (such as selenium and zinc) and plant compounds called phytochemicals. You'll find them in fruit and vegetables, seeds, nuts, oils, whole grains, beans and lentils – foods that are at the heart of the 14-day mini-detox diet. Many studies have indicated that a diet rich in these antioxidant foods protects against heart disease and cancer, delays ageing and prevents cataracts.

Phytonutrients

Phytonutrients are compounds found naturally in fruit, vegetables, whole grains, beans, lentils and soya products – also foods that feature heavily in the 14-day mini-detox diet. They include bioflavanoids, polyphenols, carotenoids, coumestrol, salicylates, sulphoramine, anthocyanins, flavanols, limonene, isoflavones and lutein. They act as powerful antioxidants that work with vitamins and minerals to protect the body from degenerative diseases (such as heart disease and cancer), boost immunity and fight harmful bacteria and viruses. There are hundreds of different types of phytochemicals and the best way to make sure you get enough of them is to eat at least five daily portions of fruits and vegetables. Aim to eat a variety of different colours – the more intense the colour, the higher the phytonutrient level will be.

CHAPTER 6
DETOX
DIET TIPS

The key to making it simple to follow the 14-day mini-detox diet is preparation. If you follow the tips in this chapter you should have no problem staying on track.

Plan your meal times

Always make time to eat. Plan when you will eat in advance and don't be tempted to schedule engagements at mealtimes. The key is to fit the rest of your schedule around your mealtimes rather than the other way round.

Organise your daily food in advance

On days when you will be away from home, take a supply of healthy snacks and mini-meals with you to eat (see below for ideas). That way you won't have to grab the nearest available sugary snack.

Prepare ahead

If you know that you will be pushed for time, prepare your meals in advance. For example, make a big bowl of salad or a huge pan of soup – enough for several portions. Keep the remainder in the fridge or freezer.

Shop wisely

Make a habit of shopping with a shopping list (see page 53). This saves shopping time and ensures that you will always have the right ingredients to hand in your kitchen.

Stock up

Have a stock of healthy staples in your store cupboard so you will always be able to prepare a quick meal at short notice. Buy canned beans, lentils and tomatoes, non-wheat pasta, quinoa, millet, nuts, seeds, rye crispbreads, oatcakes and dried fruit.

Choose the right time for it

I suggest that you pick a fortnight during which you will have few commitments or distractions so that you can keep focused on your eating plan. Otherwise, you may find that if you take on too many new challenges and become overstressed, your resolve to eat properly weakens. We all know how easy it is to reach for a chocolate bar or a glass of wine when we're tired, stressed or angry!

One week or two?

Ideally, you should follow the menu plan for fourteen days. If you can only manage seven days you'll still benefit, but if you can continue longer then you will notice a bigger improvement in your energy levels, skin complexion and body shape. Although weight loss is not the major objective of this plan, you may find that you shed a few surplus pounds once you cut out all those high-fat, sugary snacks. By filling up on fibre-packed nutritious foods instead, you can expect to lose up to 1kg (2lb) per week.

Be flexible

Use this 14-day menu plan as a base for developing your own eating plan. While the daily menus have been carefully balanced to provide the right proportions of nutrients to keep you healthy, it is possible to swap meals between different days. For example, you may prefer to have the lunch suggested for day 7 on day 1 instead.

Eat in tune with your body

The lunches and evening meals are also interchangeable. So, if you prefer to have your main meal at lunchtime and the suggested lunch in the evening, it's quite OK to swap the meals around.

Change a few ingredients

Most of the recipes can be adapted slightly according to which food you have to hand. You don't have to stick rigidly to the stated ingredients. For example, with the recipe for roasted winter vegetables (see recipe, page 70) you may use other vegetables instead of those suggested in the recipe.

Keep favourite recipes

Feel free to adapt your favourite recipes to fit in with the detox principles. By omitting or substituting a few ingredients in your own recipe, you can incorporate it into the 14-day mini-detox diet. This is useful when you have to cook for your family or friends. Alternatively, take out your portion before adding, say, the cheese or meat to the remainder of the dish for everyone else. Easy!

Keep changing

Whether you decide to use all of the recipes in this eating plan or you include some of your own, remember to vary the foods you eat daily. The more varied your diet overall, the more likely you are to get all the vitamins, minerals and phytonutrients you need. It may seem easier to begin with to stick to the same meals day after day, but you could end up missing out on some nutrients.

Listen to your body

You'll notice that this eating plan does not state precise amounts for some of the foods; for example, accompanying rice or fresh fruit. That's because we all have different energy and nutritional needs and, therefore, should eat different quantities of food. Listen to your body and respond to your appetite. Eat when you are hungry, eat only as much as your body needs – and no more – and then stop eating when you are satisfied. Believe me, this really works – provided you are choosing naturally filling nutrient-packed foods (like vegetables, fruit and whole grains) and not high-calorie sugary foods.

Get ahead

To make life easier, you may wish to prepare some of the dishes in advance or cook larger amounts so that you have a meal ready – in the fridge or freezer – when you are more pressed for time. Try to prepare vegetables, salads and fruit salads just before you eat them, though, as they start to lose their vitamins through oxidation once they are cut.

Eating at work

Take healthy snacks and easy light meals with you to work. That way you won't have to rely on the choice in the canteen or local sandwich bar. Here are a few healthy ideas:

- Freshly squeezed juice
- Dips e.g. guacamole, hummus (see recipes, pages 90, 65)
- Rye crackers, rice cakes, oatcakes
- Non-wheat bread
- Soup in a flask
- Small packets of dried (unsulphured) fruit e.g. apricots, mangos, sultanas
- Nuts e.g. almonds, Brazils, walnuts
- Seeds e.g. sesame, sunflower
- Sesame snaps (occasional)

Eating on the move

It is often difficult to eat healthily when you spend a lot of your time travelling. Don't be tempted to skip meals or grab fast foods and salty snacks. Here are some ideas for healthy snacks for eating in cars, trains, buses and planes:

- A small bag of unsalted nuts, e.g. almonds, cashews
- A piece of fresh fruit, e.g. apple, banana, grapes
- Bottle of mineral water
- Mini-boxes of raisins
- Fruit bar or liquorice bar (occasional)
- Prepared vegetable sticks e.g. carrots, peppers and celery
- Rye crackers and oatcakes
- Sandwich made from rye bread

Eating out

Eating out should be enjoyable, so don't feel you have to deprive yourself and feel miserable. Don't try to stick to the diet plan completely, but just choose the healthier options wherever you can. Choose vegetable-based dishes, salads or rice dishes and try to avoid anything fried, creamy sauces, meat, bread and dairy products. If you do stray from the detox rules, don't feel guilty but resume the diet plan the next day.

Family meals

Many of the meals and recipes can easily be adapted to suit the needs and tastes of other family members. You can increase their portion sizes and add a few extras, such as poultry, fish or low-fat dairy products, to meet their requirements. You may find that your other half becomes a willing convert!

Note: **This detox diet is unsuitable for children under eighteen,** because they are still growing and developing.

CHAPTER 7

DETOX SUPERFOODS

Apples

Apples contain vitamin C – a great immunity booster – and quercetin, an antioxidant that protects against cancer. Apples are also rich in pectin, a soluble type of fibre that helps lower blood-cholesterol levels and keeps the intestines and bowel working properly.

Avocados

Avocados are rich in vitamin E and alphacarotene, both powerful antioxidants that help prevent furring of the arteries and heart disease. They also contain monounsaturated fat, which lowers blood cholesterol and heart-disease risk, as well as the essential omega-6 fats, which promote healthy skin.

Beans and lentils

Beans and lentils contain a good balance of protein and complex carbohydrates, and provide sustained energy. They are rich in sterols (plant compounds) and soluble fibre, both of which help lower blood cholesterol, as well as B-vitamins, magnesium, zinc and iron.

Broccoli

Broccoli, along with other cruciferous vegetables – cauliflower, cabbage, Brussels sprouts and spinach – are powerful detoxifiers. They contain phytonutrients called glucosinolates, which can fight cancer, especially of the bowel, breast, lungs and liver.

Carrots

Carrots are rich in the antioxidants, alphacarotene and betacarotene, which help to protect against lung cancer. These nutrients also help to boost immunity, promote healthier skin and maintain good eyesight.

Fennel

Fennel helps stimulate the body's natural detoxifying organs, including the liver. It is also good for the digestive system and its high potassium content helps rebalance the body's fluid levels.

Garlic

Garlic contains allicin, an antioxidant nutrient that helps protect the body from heart disease, high blood pressure, high blood-cholesterol levels and colon cancer. It can also bind with toxins in the body to render them harmless and promote their excretion. In addition it has antiviral and antibacterial actions.

Kiwi fruit

Kiwi fruit are super-rich in vitamin C, an antioxidant that helps fight cancer and potentially harmful free radicals. It also boosts the immune system and strengthens the blood vessels.

Mangos

Mangos are rich in betacarotene and vitamin C, two powerful anti-oxidants that help ward off colds and reduce the risk of cancer and heart disease. They are also good sources of vitamin E, fibre and potassium.

Pumpkin seeds

Pumpkin seeds and their oil contain a healthy balance of the essential omega-3 and omega-6 oils, which help to protect against heart disease and stroke. Omega-3-rich foods can reduce joint pain and stiffness, improve immunity and promote healthy skin.

Strawberries

Strawberries are rich in vitamin C which not only boosts immunity but also fights free radicals and helps prevent heart disease and cancer. They also contain ellagic acid, an antioxidant with powerful anti-cancer effects.

Watercress

Watercress is rich in chlorophyll, a dark-green pigment, which helps make healthy blood cells and improves circulation. It boosts levels of detoxifying enzymes in the liver.

CHAPTER 8
SHOPPING LIST

Use the following shopping list as a basis for developing your own list. It includes most of the foods you'll be eating over the next fourteen days so gives you a good idea of the types of products to look out for in the shops. Add or take off foods according to the menus you select and your own food preferences.

Drinks

Mineral water
Rooibos tea
Pure fruit juice

Herbal or fruit teas
Green tea
Vegetable juice

Fruit

Apples
Apricots
Avocados
Bananas

Blackberries
Blueberries
Cherries
Clementines

Dates
Dried apricots
Figs
Grapefruit
Kiwi fruit
Lemons
Limes
Mangos
Melons
Olives
Papayas
Peaches

Pears
Pineapples
Plums
Raisins
Raspberries
Rhubarb
Satsumas
Strawberries
Sultanas
Tomatoes
Watermelon

Vegetables

Asparagus
Baby corn
Broccoli
Cabbages
Cauliflowers
Celery
Courgettes
Cucumbers
Fennel
Garlic
Green beans
Lamb's lettuce
Lettuce
Mangetout
Mixed salad leaves

Mushrooms
Onions
Peas (fresh or frozen)
Peppers – red, yellow, orange or green
Potatoes
Pumpkin
Rocket
Spinach
Spring onions
Squash
Sugar-snap peas
Sweet potatoes
Watercress

Grains

Millet (whole grain)
Millet flakes
Non-wheat pasta (e.g. corn, rice, millet)
Oats
Rice flour
Quinoa
Whole-grain (brown) rice

Breads and Crispbreads

Oatcakes
Pumpernickel bread
Rice cakes
Rye bread
Rye crackers
Wheat-free bread

Beans and Lentils

Select either tinned or dried versions of:
Black-eyed beans
Butter beans
Chickpeas
Flageolet beans
Lentils (red, green, brown)
Red kidney beans
Sprouted beans e.g. mung, alfalfa

Nuts and seeds

Select unsalted whole, flaked or groundnuts, such as:
Almonds
Brazils
Cashews
Hazelnuts
Linseeds (flaxseeds)
Peanuts
Pecans
Pine nuts
Pumpkin seeds
Sesame seeds
Sunflower seeds
Walnuts

Healthy oils

Dairy-free spread
Linseed (flaxseed) oil
Omega-3 spread
Pumpkinseed oil
Sesame oil
Sweet almond oil

Extra-virgin olive oil
Olive oil spread
Omega-3-rich oils
Rapeseed oil
Sunflower oil
Walnut oil

Non-dairy foods

Almond milk
Rice milk
Soya yoghurt

Coconut milk
Soya milk
Tofu

Other

Selection of fresh and dried herbs (e.g. basil, parsley, mint, coriander)
Spices (e.g. cinnamon, ground cumin or coriander)
Chillies
Dijon or whole-grain mustard
Fresh ginger
Light soy sauce
Honey
Cider, red wine or balsamic vinegar

CHAPTER 9
KEEP IT GOING FOR 14 DAYS – AND BEYOND

The 14-day mini-detox diet is designed to kick-start some good habits that will get you off to a healthy start. After a fortnight you'll look and feel a hundred per cent better. Continue healthy eating habits for longer and you'll reap more benefits.

The chances are that you will want to maintain the new healthier you. Going back to old eating habits would undo all that good work and you would lose many of the benefits you gained.

Try to incorporate the main elements from this 14-day mini-detox diet into your regular diet. Of course, you need not stick to the detox principles as rigidly as you have been. You are allowed a little more room for manoeuvre now that you have rid your body of excessive toxins; follow these guidelines:

- Keep to the healthy eating principles at least eighty per cent of the time.
- Reintroduce certain foods that you have missed to fill the remaining twenty per cent. For example, you may wish to include ordinary wheat bread or a wheat breakfast cereal in your diet. That should be fine provided you continue to listen to your body. If you notice any symptoms, such as bloating or sluggishness, then cut back or eliminate.
- Avoid or minimise heavily processed foods for the first week or so. After this time, if you really want some chocolate, or a bit of cake or whatever, have some. Just don't overdo it! You may find that you no longer crave the foods you used to or that they no longer make you feel satisfied.
- It's best to reintroduce foods one at a time rather than eating them all at once. That way, you will be able to work out which one(s) causes you unpleasant symptoms. Keep a food diary, if you can, noting down what you eat and how you feel.
- Vary your regular diet by incorporating more varieties of grains (rye, whole wheat, whole-grain rice, corn, quinoa and millet), lean protein foods (fish, chicken, eggs, tofu, Quorn and different beans and lentils), and dairy foods (skimmed milk, soya, rice, oat or almond milk, yoghurt or soya 'yoghurt'). If you suspect a food allergy or intolerance (e.g. dairy or gluten) you should consult a qualified nutritional practitioner for professional advice.
- Allow yourself those little indulgences – whether it's chocolate, cheese or wine – without feeling guilty. Most people who have completed a detox diet find that their craving is satisfied after eating or drinking only a very small amount. It is surprising how your taste buds change after eating super-healthily for fourteen days! Where

before you may have eaten a whole chocolate bar (or more!), you may well find that a couple of squares of chocolate do the trick.

■ Continue to listen to your body. If a certain food or drink doesn't feel 'right' or simply doesn't appeal, then don't have it. You should now be much more in tune with your body than you were fourteen days ago. Eat what your body really needs, savour your food and enjoy life!

Can I follow the diet plan longer than 14 days?

You should quickly start to see and feel results after a week – you may find that you sleep better, have more energy or lose excess weight – but it normally takes 28 days to really reap the benefits. You may continue to follow the diet programme longer than 14 days if you wish, provided you are feeling well and you include a *wide variety* of foods from the permitted list.

For more diet and recipe ideas, see *Carol Vorderman's Detox for Life* (Virgin Books, £10.99), *Carol Vorderman's Summer Detox* (Virgin Books, £10.99), and *Carol Vorderman's Detox Recipes* (Virgin Books, £10.99).

How often should I follow the 14-day detox diet plan?

Clearly, this is not a quick-fix diet that you stick to for a while only to lapse back to old ways. The aim is to adapt the principles of the detox diet to your long-term eating habits.

However, no one's perfect, and sometimes it is easy to let good habits slide a little. For example, during stressful periods, on holiday or during the Christmas festivities, you may not eat as healthily as usual. Toxins may begin to accumulate and your system gets overworked again. You will start to recognise those symptoms of toxin build-up.

That's the time to stock up and go back on the 14-day mini-detox diet. You may need to do this once every six months or once a year, for example, as part of your New Year's resolution. Do it whenever you feel the time is right for you.

It may not always be necessary to do the full 14-day detox. You may feel that a week is enough to restore your energy and health. You may even feel that all you need is to cut back on certain foods or drinks for a while, for example wheat, alcohol or coffee. The main message is: listen to your body and respond accordingly.

CHAPTER 10
THE 14-DAY
EATING PLAN

BREAKFAST

Porridge with raisins and apricots

LUNCH

Slice of rye (or other non-wheat) bread

Hummus

Crudités, e.g. carrot, cucumber, red pepper, cherry tomatoes, celery

1 portion (125g/4oz) fresh fruit (e.g. 2 plums, 1 apple)

EVENING MEAL

Bean Provençale with black olives

3 tablespoons (45ml) cooked brown rice

Orange and kiwi fruit salad

SNACKS

4 Brazil nuts

1 banana

day 1

PORRIDGE WITH RAISINS AND APRICOTS

MAKES 1 SERVING

40g (1½oz) rolled porridge oats
60ml (2fl oz) soya, rice, sesame or almond milk
60ml (2fl oz) water
1 tablespoon (15ml) raisins
4 ready-to-eat apricots
1 teaspoon (5ml) honey

Mix the oats, milk and water in a saucepan. Bring to the boil and simmer for 4 to 5 minutes, stirring frequently.

Meanwhile, snip the apricots into bite-sized pieces and add them to the cooked porridge along with the raisins.

Spoon into bowls and drizzle the honey on top.

HUMMUS

MAKES 4 SERVINGS

400g (14oz) tinned chickpeas
2 garlic cloves, crushed
2 tablespoons (30ml) extra-virgin olive oil
120ml (4fl oz) tahini (sesame seed paste)
Juice of 1 lemon
2–4 tablespoons (30–60ml) water
A little low-sodium salt and freshly ground black pepper
Pinch of paprika or cayenne pepper

Drain and rinse the chickpeas. Put them in a food processor or blender with the remaining ingredients, apart from the paprika. Process to a smooth paste.

Add extra water if necessary to give the desired consistency. Adjust the seasoning to taste.

Spoon into a serving dish. Pour over a little olive oil and sprinkle with cayenne or paprika. Chill in the fridge for at least 2 hours before serving.

BEAN PROVENÇALE WITH BLACK OLIVES

MAKES 2 SERVINGS

1 tablespoon (15ml) extra-virgin olive oil
1 onion, sliced
Half a red pepper, deseeded and sliced
Half a green pepper, deseeded and sliced
1 garlic clove, crushed
1 courgette, trimmed and sliced
200g (7oz) tinned chopped tomatoes
200g (7oz) tinned cannellini beans or butter beans
1 tablespoon (15ml) tomato paste
1 teaspoon (5ml) dried oregano or basil
25g (1oz) black olives
A little low-sodium salt and freshly ground black pepper
A small handful of fresh parsley or basil leaves, chopped

Heat the olive oil in a heavy-based pan and sauté the onions and peppers over a moderate heat until soft. Add the garlic and courgettes and continue cooking for a further 5 minutes, stirring occasionally.

Add the tomatoes, beans, tomato paste and dried herbs. Cover and simmer for 15 to 20 minutes, adding the olives 5 minutes before the end of the cooking time. Season with the low-sodium salt and black pepper. Serve sprinkled with the parsley or basil leaves.

ORANGE AND KIWI FRUIT SALAD

MAKES 2 SERVINGS

2 oranges
2 kiwi fruit
1 teaspoon (5ml) orange flower water (or orange juice)
Manuka honey to taste

Carefully remove the peel and pith from the oranges then cut into segments. Put in a bowl.

Peel the kiwi fruit and slice thinly. Add to the bowl.

Add the orange flower water (or orange juice) and honey to taste and mix gently.

orange
and kiwi fruit salad

BREAKFAST

Slice of toast – rye bread or other non-wheat bread

with olive oil spread and honey

One portion (125g/4oz) fresh fruit

(e.g. 1 orange, 2 satsumas, half a grapefruit)

LUNCH

Carrot soup with fresh coriander

Slice of rye (or other non-wheat) bread with a little olive oil spread

1 portion (125g/4oz) fresh fruit (e.g. 2 plums, 1 apple)

EVENING MEAL

Roasted winter vegetables with toasted pumpkin seeds

3 tablespoons (45ml) cooked quinoa,

cooked according to packet instructions

SNACKS

2 rice cakes topped with 2 teaspoons (10ml) peanut butter

125g (4oz) fresh fruit

CARROT SOUP WITH FRESH CORIANDER

MAKES 2 SERVINGS

1 tablespoon (15ml) extra-virgin olive oil
1 small onion, finely sliced
1 garlic clove, crushed
4 carrots, sliced
500ml (16fl oz) vegetable stock
1 bay leaf
A little low-sodium salt and freshly ground black pepper
A handful of fresh coriander, roughly chopped

Heat the olive oil in a heavy-based saucepan over a moderate heat. Add the onion and sauté gently for about 5 minutes until it is translucent.

Add the garlic and cook for a further 1 to 2 minutes. Add the carrots, stock and bay leaf to the pan, stir, then bring to the boil. Simmer for 15 minutes or until the vegetables are tender.

Allow the soup to cool slightly for a couple of minutes. Remove and discard the bay leaf. Liquidise the soup using a hand blender or conventional blender. Season to taste with low-sodium salt and pepper, then stir in the fresh coriander.

ROASTED WINTER VEGETABLES
WITH TOASTED PUMPKIN SEEDS

You can use any seasonal vegetables of your choice

MAKES 2 SERVINGS

225g (8oz) pumpkin, peeled and thickly sliced
1 carrot, peeled and halved
2 parsnips, peeled and cut into quarters
1 small sweet potato, peeled and sliced
Half a small swede, peeled and cut into wedges
Few sprigs of rosemary
1 garlic clove, crushed
Salt and freshly ground black pepper
1 tablespoon (15ml) olive oil
2 tablespoons (30ml) pumpkin seeds

Prepare the vegetables and place in a large roasting tin.

Place the herbs between the vegetables and sprinkle with the crushed garlic and pepper. Drizzle over the oil and turn the vegetables gently so they are coated in a little oil.

Roast in a pre-heated oven at 200C/400F/gas mark 6 for 30 to 40 minutes until the vegetables are tender.

Meanwhile lightly toast the pumpkin seeds on a baking tray for approximately 5 minutes in the oven. Allow to cool, then scatter over the roasted vegetables just before serving.

BREAKFAST

Muesli with toasted nuts and seeds

LUNCH

Chickpea, coriander and lime salad

One portion (125g/4oz) fruit

(e.g. 1 orange, 2 clementines, a handful of grapes)

EVENING MEAL

Noodle and tofu stir-fry

Melon with strawberries and mint

SNACKS

1 small pot (150ml/5fl oz) plain soya yoghurt or natural

bio-yoghurt mixed with 125g (4oz) chopped fresh fruit

(e.g. strawberries, banana or blueberries)

A glass of fresh fruit juice

MUESLI WITH TOASTED NUTS AND SEEDS

MAKES 1 SERVING

40g (1½oz) millet or rice flakes
85ml (3fl oz) chilled fruit juice or rice, soya, almond or oat milk
2 teaspoons (10ml) sunflower seeds, lightly toasted
2 teaspoons (10ml) pumpkin seeds, lightly toasted
1 tablespoon (15ml) toasted flaked almonds
1 tablespoon (15ml) chopped toasted hazelnuts
1 tablespoon (15ml) raisins or sultanas
Fresh fruit, e.g. grated apple, sliced banana, strawberries
    (optional)

Put the cereal flakes in a bowl and pour the juice or milk over them.
Leave to soak for 15 minutes.

Add the seeds, nuts and raisins and mix the ingredients together.
Serve in individual bowls, topped with the fresh fruit (if liked).

CHICKPEA, CORIANDER AND LIME SALAD

MAKES 2 SERVINGS

275g (9oz) cooked chickpeas (or use a 400g can chickpeas,
   drained and rinsed)
Half a red onion, thinly sliced
Half a red pepper, finely chopped
1 tablespoon (15ml) fresh coriander, chopped
1 garlic clove, crushed
1 tablespoon (15ml) olive oil
Juice of 1 lime

Drain and rinse the chickpeas. Combine with the sliced onion,
chopped pepper and chopped coriander.

In a screw-top jar, mix together the crushed garlic, olive oil and lime
juice. Pour over the chickpea salad, mix well and chill in the fridge.
This is best prepared at least 2 hours in advance before eating so the
chickpeas have time to absorb the flavours.

NOODLE AND TOFU STIR-FRY

MAKES 2 SERVINGS

Juice of 1 lime (or lemon)
2 tablespoons (30ml) water
2 garlic cloves, crushed
175g (6oz) firm tofu, cubed
85g (3oz) rice noodles
1 tablespoon (15ml) olive or sesame oil
2.5cm (1 inch) piece fresh ginger, chopped
4 spring onions, chopped
225g (8oz) mushrooms, sliced
125g (4oz) bean sprouts
1 teaspoon (5ml) cornflour

Mix the lime (or lemon) juice, water and half the garlic in a small
shallow dish. Add the tofu, stir to coat in the marinade and set aside
for 30 minutes.

Cook the noodles in a saucepan according to the instructions on the
packet. Drain.

Heat the oil in a wok and stir-fry the remaining garlic and ginger
for 1 minute. Add the spring onions, mushrooms and bean sprouts,
and stir-fry for 2 minutes. Add the drained noodles and cook a
further minute.

Drain the tofu, reserving the marinade, and add to the vegetables and noodles. Blend the reserved marinade with the cornflour to make a smooth paste, then pour over the vegetables. Continue cooking, stirring constantly until the sauce has thickened. Transfer onto a serving dish.

noodle and tofu stir-fry

MELON WITH STRAWBERRIES AND MINT

MAKES 2 SERVINGS

125g (4oz) strawberries
2 sprigs of mint
8 blanched almonds
1 small Ogen or galia melon

Cut the strawberries into halves or quarters and place in a bowl.
Roughly tear the mint leaves and add to the strawberries.

Add the almonds.

Cut the melon in half. Scoop out the seeds and fill the cavities with
the strawberries.

BREAKFAST

Strawberry banana smoothie

LUNCH

1 small baked potato with a drizzle of extra-virgin olive oil
or flaxseed oil
1 or 2 tablespoons (15–30ml) hummus or guacamole
(ready-bought or see recipes, pages 65, 90)
Mixed salad leaves
125g (4oz) fresh fruit (e.g. peach, orange or kiwi fruit)

EVENING MEAL

Pasta with broccoli and pine nuts
Warm berry compote with cinnamon

SNACKS

125g (4oz) fresh fruit (e.g. plums, peach or nectarine)
1 pot plain soya yoghurt or natural bio-yoghurt
mixed with 3 chopped dried apricots

STRAWBERRY BANANA SMOOTHIE

MAKES 1

125ml (4fl oz) orange juice
60g (2oz) strawberries
1 banana, frozen and sliced *

Place the orange juice, strawberries and frozen banana slices in a
smoothie maker, blender or food processor and process until smooth
and thick. Serve immediately.

* Peel bananas, place in a plastic bag and freeze.

PASTA WITH BROCCOLI AND PINE NUTS

MAKES 2 SERVINGS

225g (8oz) broccoli
1 tablespoon (15ml) extra-virgin olive oil
1 small onion, chopped
1 garlic clove, crushed
200g (7oz) canned chopped tomatoes
1 tablespoon (15ml) pine nuts
40g (1½oz) sultanas
125g (4oz) non-wheat pasta
Low-sodium salt and freshly ground black pepper

Divide the broccoli into florets and briefly cook in a pan of boiling water for 3 to 4 minutes. Drain well and keep warm.

Heat the olive oil in a pan and cook the onion and garlic for 5 minutes until the onion is soft but not brown. Add the tomatoes and season with low-sodium salt and pepper and simmer for a few minutes. Add the broccoli and sultanas.

Toast the pine nuts in a dry pan for a minute or two until they start to turn golden.

Cook the pasta in a large pan of boiling water according to the directions on the packet.

Drain and transfer to a serving dish. Mix with the broccoli mixture and the pine nuts.

WARM BERRY COMPOTE WITH CINNAMON

MAKES 2 SERVINGS

225g (8oz) mixed fresh or frozen berries, e.g. raspberries,
    blackberries, strawberries, cranberries, blueberries
2 tablespoons (30ml) honey
1 cinnamon stick
2 slices orange

Put the fruit into a saucepan and add the honey, cinnamon stick and orange slices. Add just enough water to cover. Bring to the boil, then reduce the heat and simmer, stirring from time to time, for 10 minutes until the liquid has reduced by half.

Allow to cool, then remove the cinnamon stick and orange slices.

BREAKFAST

Plain soya or bio-yoghurt with fruit

(shop-bought or home-made: see recipe, page 82)

One portion (125g/4oz) fresh fruit,

e.g. 1 banana, 2 kiwi fruit, 2 clementines

LUNCH

Root vegetable soup

Slice of rye (or other non-wheat) bread or 2 rye or rice crackers

1 portion (125g/4oz) fresh fruit

(e.g. strawberries, raspberries or blueberries)

EVENING MEAL

Chickpeas with butternut squash and tomatoes

A medium jacket potato with a teaspoon (5ml) olive oil

or omega-3 spread

SNACKS

Small handful of toasted seeds

(e.g. pumpkin, sunflower or sesame seeds)

125g (4oz) fresh fruit (e.g. 1 orange, 2 satsumas, 2 kiwi fruit)

HOME-MADE SOYA YOGHURT WITH FRUIT

Making your own yoghurt is far easier than you might imagine. It's nutritious and, unlike most shop-bought brands, is not loaded with sugar and artificial additives. Soya is rich in protein and calcium and a regular daily intake can help protect against breast cancer.

600ml (1 pint) soya milk
1 tablespoon (15ml) live natural soya yoghurt
4 tablespoons (60ml) soya milk powder (optional)
3 tablespoons (45ml) puréed fresh fruit, pure fruit compote or fruit
    spread

Heat the soya milk in a saucepan until it reaches boiling point. Remove from the heat and allow to cool.

When tepid, mix in the soya yoghurt and soya milk powder.

Pour into a clean vacuum flask or yoghurt maker. Place the vacuum flask in a warm place for about 8 hours or overnight. Pour out into a clean bowl and place in the fridge until firm.

Stir in the puréed fruit, fruit compote or spread.

ROOT VEGETABLE SOUP

MAKES 2 SERVINGS

1 tablespoon (15ml) extra virgin olive oil
1 small onion, finely sliced
225g (8oz – approx 3) carrots, sliced
125g (4oz – approx 1) parsnips, diced
125g (4oz) swede, diced
500ml (¾ pint) vegetable stock
1 bay leaf
A little low-sodium salt and freshly ground black pepper

Heat the olive oil in a heavy-based saucepan over a moderate heat. Add the onion and sauté gently for about 5 minutes until it is translucent.

Add the carrots, parsnips and swede to the pan and mix well. Cook gently over a moderately low heat for 5 minutes, stirring occasionally, until the vegetables soften a little.

Add the stock and bay leaf and bring to the boil. Simmer for 15 minutes or until the vegetables are tender.

Allow the soup to cool slightly for a couple of minutes. Remove and discard the bay leaf. Liquidise the soup using a hand blender or conventional blender. Season to taste with salt and pepper.

CHICKPEAS WITH BUTTERNUT SQUASH AND TOMATOES

MAKES 2 SERVINGS

1 tablespoon (15ml) extra-virgin olive oil
1 onion, chopped
Half a red pepper, deseeded and chopped
125g (4oz) butternut squash, peeled and chopped
200g (7oz) tinned chopped tomatoes
150ml (4fl oz) vegetable stock
200g (7oz) tinned chickpeas, drained and rinsed

Heat the oil in a heavy-based pan, add the onion and peppers and cook over a moderate heat for 5 minutes.

Add the squash, tomatoes, vegetable stock and chickpeas, stir, then bring to the boil. Lower the heat and simmer for 20 minutes, stirring occasionally.

Serve with the jacket potato.

BREAKFAST

Muesli with fruit and nuts

LUNCH

Baked sweet potato, drizzle of extra-virgin olive oil or walnut oil

Ratatouille

Bowl of fresh fruit, e.g. apple slices and grapes

EVENING MEAL

Vegetable and lentil curry

3 tablespoons (45ml) cooked brown rice

SNACKS

125g (4oz) fresh fruit (e.g. 1 peach or 2 kiwi fruit)

Carrot, celery and cucumber sticks dipped in a little hummus

MUESLI WITH FRUIT AND NUTS

MAKES 1 SERVING

40g (1½oz) porridge oats, millet or rice flakes
85ml (3fl oz) soya, rice, almond or oat milk
1 tablespoon (15ml) raisins or sultanas
1 tablespoon (15ml) toasted flaked almonds or chopped hazelnuts
2 teaspoons (10ml) ground linseeds (optional)
1 apple, peeled and grated, or other fresh fruit, e.g. banana,
    strawberries

In a large bowl, mix together the oats (or other flakes), milk, dried fruit,
nuts and ground linseeds. Cover and leave overnight in the fridge. To
serve, stir in the grated apple or other fruit. Spoon into cereal bowls.

muesli
with fruit
and nuts

RATATOUILLE

MAKES 2 SERVINGS

1–2 tablespoons (15–30ml) extra-virgin olive oil
1 onion, peeled and chopped
Half each of red, yellow and green peppers, deseeded and sliced
1 clove of garlic, crushed
1 large courgette, sliced
Half an aubergine, diced
350g (12oz) tomatoes, skinned and chopped (or use a 400g can
    tomatoes)
Sea salt and freshly ground black pepper
1 tablespoon (15ml) chopped fresh parsley

Heat the oil in a large saucepan. Add the onions and peppers and
cook gently for 5 minutes.

Add the garlic, courgettes, aubergine and tomatoes. Stir, then cover
and cook over a low heat for 20 to 25 minutes until all the vegetables
are tender.

Season to taste with salt and freshly ground black pepper and sprinkle
with the chopped parsley. Serve hot or cold.

VEGETABLE AND LENTIL CURRY

MAKES 2 SERVINGS

2 tablespoons (30ml) water or vegetable stock
1 small onion, sliced
Half a teaspoon (2.5ml) of each: cumin, coriander, turmeric and
    chilli powder (alternatively, use 2 teaspoons (10ml) of curry
    powder)
1 garlic clove, crushed
125g (4oz) red lentils
400ml (12fl oz) water
450g (1lb) vegetables of your choice: cauliflower, courgettes,
    mushrooms, okra, carrots, tomatoes

Sauté the onion in the water or stock for 5 minutes.

Add the spices and the garlic and continue cooking for 2 minutes.

Add the red lentils, cover and simmer for 10 minutes. Add the
vegetables and continue cooking for 20 minutes or until the
vegetables are just tender.

BREAKFAST

Plate of fresh fruit – at least 2 portions,

e.g. satsumas, pears, grapes, strawberries, bananas

Small pot of soya or bio-yoghurt mixed with 1 tablespoon (15ml)

toasted nuts (e.g. almonds, cashews) or seeds

LUNCH

Guacamole (avocado dip)

Slice of rye (or non-wheat) bread

Crudités, e.g. carrot, cucumber, red pepper, cherry tomatoes, celery

One portion (125g/4oz) fresh fruit, e.g. 2 kiwi fruit; 2 satsumas

EVENING MEAL

Vegetable chilli

3 tablespoons (45ml) cooked quinoa

Plums with orange and mint

SNACKS

2 rice crackers (rice cakes) topped with

2 teaspoons (10ml) peanut butter

A glass of fresh fruit juice

GUACAMOLE (AVOCADO DIP)

MAKES 2 SERVINGS

1 ripe avocado
1 tablespoon (15ml) lemon or lime juice
Half a small red onion, finely chopped
1 small garlic clove, crushed
1 medium tomato, skinned and chopped
Half a fresh green chilli, deseeded and chopped (optional)
1 tablespoon (15ml) fresh coriander, finely chopped
Sea salt and freshly ground black pepper
Coriander sprigs to serve

Halve each avocado; remove the stone and scoop out the flesh.
Mash the avocado flesh with the lemon or lime juice, using a fork.

Add the remaining ingredients, mixing well. Check the seasoning,
adding a little more black pepper or lemon juice if necessary.

Spoon into a serving dish, cover and chill. Garnish with the coriander
sprigs before serving.

guacamole

VEGETABLE CHILLI

MAKES 2 SERVINGS

1 small onion, chopped
Half a green pepper, chopped
1 celery stick, sliced
85ml (3fl oz) water
1 garlic clove, crushed
200g (7oz) tinned chopped tomatoes
1 teaspoon (5ml) tomato paste
Half a vegetable bouillon cube
1 teaspoon (5ml) chopped fresh parsley
Half a teaspoon (2.5ml) chilli powder, or to taste
Pinch of ground cumin
400g (14oz) tinned red kidney beans, drained and rinsed

Combine the onion, pepper, celery, water and garlic in large saucepan.
Cook over a medium–high heat, stirring occasionally, for 6 to 8
minutes or until the vegetables are tender.

Add the tomatoes, tomato paste, bouillon, parsley, chilli powder and
cumin; stir well. Stir in the beans. Bring to the boil, cover, and then
reduce the heat and simmer, stirring occasionally, for 45 minutes.

PLUMS WITH ORANGE AND MINT

MAKES 2 SERVINGS

225g (8oz) purple plums
60ml (2fl oz) fresh orange juice
A few fresh mint leaves, torn
A little honey or maple syrup (optional)

Halve the plums and remove the stones. Cut them into thin slices and place in a bowl.

Add the remaining ingredients and toss well.

Cover and chill in the fridge, stirring occasionally, for at least 2 hours.

BREAKFAST

Banana porridge with honey

LUNCH

Tomato and vegetable soup

Slice of rye (or other non-wheat) bread with a little olive oil spread

1 portion (125g/4oz) fresh fruit (e.g. 2 plums, 1 apple)

EVENING MEAL

Quinoa and rice with pumpkin seeds

Fresh fruit medley

SNACKS

125g (4oz) fresh fruit (e.g. apple, pear or banana)

1 small pot (150ml/5fl oz) plain soya yoghurt or natural bio-yoghurt

mixed with 1 tablespoon (15ml) muesli

BANANA PORRIDGE WITH HONEY

MAKES 1 SERVING

40g (1½oz) rolled porridge oats
85ml (3fl oz) soya, rice, sesame or almond milk
85ml (3fl oz) water
1 teaspoon (5ml) linseed (flaxseed) oil (optional)
1 tablespoon (15ml) raisins
1 tablespoon (15ml) ground almonds
A few toasted pumpkin seeds
Half a banana, peeled and sliced
1 teaspoon (5ml) honey

Mix the oats, milk and water in a saucepan. Bring to the boil and simmer for 4 to 5 minutes, stirring frequently.

Stir in the linseed (flaxseed) oil (if using), raisins, almonds and seeds.

Spoon into bowls and serve topped with the sliced banana and honey.

banana
porridge
with honey

TOMATO AND VEGETABLE SOUP

MAKES 2 SERVINGS

500ml (16fl oz) vegetable stock
300ml (½ pint) passata (smooth-sieved tomatoes)
1 onion, chopped
1 garlic clove, crushed
1 carrot, chopped
1 small courgette, trimmed and sliced
60g (2oz) fine green beans
60g (2oz) frozen peas
60g (2oz) frozen broad beans
1 teaspoon (5ml) dried basil
1 tablespoon (15ml) extra virgin olive or flaxseed oil

Bring the vegetable stock and passata to the boil in a large saucepan.
Add the onion, garlic and carrot. Lower the heat, cover and simmer
for 15 minutes.

Add the courgette, green beans, peas, broad beans and basil,
and continue cooking for a further 5 minutes or until the vegetables
are tender.

Turn off the heat then stir in the oil. Serve the soup hot in individual
bowls.

QUINOA* AND RICE WITH PUMPKIN SEEDS

MAKES 2 SERVINGS

1 tablespoon (15ml) extra-virgin olive oil
1 small red onion, chopped
60g (2oz) brown rice
60g (2oz) quinoa
300ml (½ pint) vegetable stock
125g (4oz) frozen peas
125g (4oz) small broccoli florets
4 tablespoons (60ml) pumpkin seeds, lightly toasted
A little low-sodium salt and freshly ground black pepper
Handful of fresh parsley, chopped

Heat the oil in a large saucepan and sauté the onion over a gentle heat for 5 minutes.

Add the rice, quinoa and stock and stir well. Bring to the boil, then reduce the heat and simmer for about 20 to 25 minutes until the liquid has been absorbed and the grains are tender.

Add the peas and broccoli and cook for a further 3 to 4 minutes.

Stir in the pumpkin seeds. Season with low-sodium salt and pepper. Stir in the parsley and serve.

* Available from health food stores. Alternatively, omit and substitute extra rice.

FRESH FRUIT MEDLEY

MAKES 2 SERVINGS

4 tablespoons (60ml) hot water
1 tablespoon (15ml) acacia (or clear) honey
1 banana, peeled and sliced
175g (6oz) berry fruits, e.g. strawberries, raspberries, blueberries
2 kiwi fruit, peeled, cut into ½-inch pieces
125g (4oz) seedless grapes

Dissolve the honey in the hot water in large bowl.

Prepare the berry fruits, slicing into bite-sized pieces, if necessary.

Add all the fruit to the honey syrup in the bowl. Toss to combine.
Cover and chill until you are ready to serve.

day 9

BREAKFAST

Nectarine and blueberry smoothie

LUNCH

1 small baked potato with a drizzle of extra-virgin olive oil

or flaxseed oil

1–2 tablespoons (15–30ml) hummus

(ready-bought or home-made: see recipe, page 65)

Mixed salad leaves

125g (4oz) fresh fruit (e.g. 1 peach, orange or 2 kiwi fruit)

EVENING MEAL

Pasta with red pepper and tomato sauce

Fresh fruit with honey, mint and lime

SNACKS

125g (4oz) fresh fruit

2 reduced-salt oatcakes topped with 2 teaspoons hummus

NECTARINE AND BLUEBERRY SMOOTHIE

MAKES 1 DRINK

1 nectarine, halved, stoned and cut into chunks
60g (2oz) blueberries
125ml (4fl oz) apple juice
A cupful of crushed ice

Place the prepared fruit, apple juice and ice in a smoothie maker,
blender or food processor and blend until smooth. Serve in a chilled
glass immediately.

nectarine
and
blueberry
smoothie

PASTA WITH RED PEPPER AND TOMATO SAUCE

MAKES 2 SERVINGS

175g (6oz) non-wheat pasta shapes
1 red pepper, deseeded and roughly chopped
2 garlic cloves, peeled
200g (7oz) tinned chopped tomatoes
A little low-sodium salt and freshly ground black pepper
A few fresh basil leaves

Bring a large pan of water to the boil and add the pasta. Cook according to the packet instructions. Drain and set aside.

Meanwhile, make the sauce. Place the chopped peppers, garlic and tomatoes in a food processor or blender with the low-sodium salt, black pepper and basil leaves. Blend until smooth, adding a little vegetable stock or water for a thinner consistency.

Stir the pepper and tomato sauce into the cooked pasta and place over a gentle heat until warmed through. Serve.

FRESH FRUIT WITH HONEY, MINT AND LIME

MAKES 2 SERVINGS

Juice and zest of 1 lime
1 tablespoon (15ml) acacia honey
1 tablespoon (15ml) chopped fresh mint
Half a cantaloupe melon, seeded
175g (6oz) strawberries, hulled and halved
2 kiwi fruit, peeled, cut into ½-inch pieces
60g (2oz) seedless grapes

Whisk lime juice and zest, honey and mint in large bowl to blend.

Using melon baler or spoon, scoop out the cantaloupe.

Add all the fruit to the honey syrup in the bowl. Toss to combine. Let it stand for 15 minutes to allow the flavours to blend. Cover and chill until you are ready to serve.

BREAKFAST

Millet or rice porridge with honey

LUNCH

Puy lentil and tomato salad with walnuts

Leafy salad (e.g. lettuce, watercress, rocket)

1 small pot (150ml/5fl oz) soya or bio-yoghurt

with 60g (2oz) berries

EVENING MEAL

Vegetable hotpot with pasta twists

Thai fruit salad

SNACKS

Smoothie

Small handful of toasted seeds

(e.g. pumpkin, sunflower or sesame seeds)

MILLET OR RICE PORRIDGE WITH HONEY

MAKES 1 SERVING

40g (1½oz) millet flakes
85ml (3fl oz) soya, rice, oat or almond milk
85ml (3fl oz) water
A few drops of vanilla extract, to taste
2 teaspoons (10ml) ground linseeds (flaxseeds)
1 teaspoon (5ml) clear honey

Mix the oats, milk and water in a saucepan. Bring to the boil and simmer for 4 to 5 minutes, stirring continuously.

Stir in the vanilla extract and ground linseeds (flaxseeds). Serve with the honey.

PUY LENTIL AND TOMATO SALAD WITH WALNUTS

MAKES 2 SERVINGS

125g (4oz) Puy lentils (or a 400g can of brown lentils)
Half a red onion, finely chopped
125g (4oz) cherry tomatoes, halved
1 tablespoon (15ml) chopped fresh parsley or mint
1–2 tablespoons (15–30ml) extra-virgin olive oil
2 teaspoons (10ml) red wine vinegar
Salt and freshly ground black pepper
25g (1oz) walnut pieces
60g (2oz) pack ready-washed salad leaves

Put the lentils in a bowl, cover with water and leave to soak for an hour. Drain.

Place in a large saucepan, cover with fresh water or vegetable stock, and bring to the boil. Reduce the heat and simmer for about an hour or until tender. Drain.

Transfer to a bowl and mix with the red onion, tomatoes and chopped herbs.

Place the olive oil and red wine vinegar in a bottle or screw-top glass jar and shake together. Pour the dressing over the lentil salad.

Toss lightly and season with salt and pepper.

Arrange the salad leaves on a serving plate, pile the lentil salad on top, then sprinkle with the walnuts.

This salad can be eaten warm or chilled.

VEGETABLE HOTPOT WITH PASTA TWISTS

MAKES 2 SERVINGS

125g (4oz) non-wheat pasta twists
1 tablespoon (15ml) extra virgin olive oil
1 garlic clove
1 small onion, chopped
1 carrot, sliced
1 courgette, trimmed and sliced
60g (2oz) button mushrooms
200g (7oz) tinned chopped tomatoes
200g (7oz) tinned borlotti or red kidney beans
150ml (¼ pint) vegetable stock
2 teaspoons (10ml) cornflour
A little low-sodium salt and freshly ground black pepper

Bring a large pan of water to the boil and cook the pasta twists according to the packet instructions. Drain.

Meanwhile, heat the olive oil in a large saucepan and sauté the garlic and onion for 3 minutes over a moderate heat. Add the carrots and cook for a further 5 minutes.

Add the courgettes and mushrooms and continue cooking for a further 3 minutes, stirring occasionally. Add the remaining ingredients except the pasta. Stir in the cooked pasta.

Bring to the boil, cover, reduce the heat and simmer for about 15 minutes until the vegetables are tender.

Mix the cornflour with a little water to make a smooth paste. Stir into the hotpot and cook for a further 2 minutes, stirring continuously, until thickened. Season with a little low-sodium salt and freshly ground black pepper.

getable
hotpot
with
pasta
twirls

THAI FRUIT SALAD

MAKES 2 SERVINGS

A quarter of a pineapple, peeled and core removed
A quarter of a honeydew melon, deseeded
1 large slice of watermelon
1 star fruit
25g (1oz) coconut flakes
1 passion fruit
Juice of 1 lime

Cut the pineapple in half lengthwise then slice across into chunks.

Peel the honeydew melon and slice into chunks.

Cut the watermelon into chunks, discarding skin and any seeds.

Cut the star fruit into four, and then slice finely.

In a large bowl toss together the pineapple, honeydew melon, watermelon, star fruit and coconut. Halve the passion fruit and scoop out the pulp into a separate bowl. Mix in the lime juice, then pour over the mixed fruit, and toss together. Cover and chill until serving.

BREAKFAST

A glass of freshly squeezed fruit juice

Fresh fruit muesli

LUNCH

1 slice of rye (or other non-wheat) bread

2 tablespoons (30ml) guacamole (see recipe, page 90)

Crudités, e.g. carrot, cucumber, red pepper, cherry tomatoes, celery

1 portion (125g/4oz) fresh fruit, e.g. 1 nectarine or pear

EVENING MEAL

Whole-grain rice pilaff with green beans and pine nuts

Green and red fruit

SNACKS

125g (4oz) fresh fruit (e.g. apple, pear or banana)

2 reduced-salt oatcakes topped with 2 teaspoons hummus

FRESH FRUIT MUESLI

MAKES 1 SERVING

40g (1½oz) cereal flakes e.g. porridge oats, rye millet and rice flakes

2 teaspoons (10ml) oat bran

2 teaspoons (10ml) seeds, e.g. sunflower, pumpkin, ground flaxseeds

2 teaspoons (10ml) flaked almonds or hazelnuts

125g (4oz) fresh fruit, e.g. strawberries, coarsely grated apple or pear, sliced kiwi

Place the cereal flakes in a serving bowl and cover with 200–250ml (7–8fl oz) water. Leave to soak overnight.

Add the oat bran and seeds and top with the fresh fruit.

Serve with soya, rice, oat or almond milk.

WHOLE-GRAIN RICE PILAFF WITH GREEN BEANS AND PINE NUTS

MAKES 2 SERVINGS

1 tablespoon (15ml) extra-virgin olive oil
1 small onion, finely chopped
1 leek, trimmed and finely sliced
1 garlic clove, crushed
Half a teaspoon (2.5ml) ground coriander
150g (5oz) whole-grain (brown) rice
450ml vegetable stock
125g (4oz) green beans, trimmed and halved
25g (1oz) pine nuts, toasted
A little low-sodium salt and freshly ground black pepper

Heat the oil in a large heavy-based pan. Add the onion, leek and garlic and cook over a moderate heat for 10 minutes until softened but not browned.

Add the coriander and brown rice and cook, stirring, for 1 minute until the grains are glossy. Add the vegetable stock and bring to the boil. Cover and simmer for 20 to 25 minutes until the liquid has been absorbed and the rice is cooked. Add the green beans during the last 5 minutes of the cooking time.

Stir in the toasted pine nuts and season with the low-sodium salt and pepper. Serve.

GREEN AND RED FRUIT

MAKES 2 SERVINGS

2 slices cantaloupe melon
125g (4oz) raspberries
125g (4oz) seedless green grapes
125ml (4fl oz) apple juice

Remove the seeds from the melon. Cut the flesh into bite-sized pieces or scoop out with a melon baller.

Combine the prepared fruit and fruit juice in a bowl.

Spoon into individual bowls and serve alone.

green and red fruit

BREAKFAST

Apricot and prune compote: soak a few dried apricots and prunes

overnight in the fridge, then stew for 5 minutes in a little water;

add a few chopped nuts (e.g. almonds, Brazils) then serve

LUNCH

Brown rice and sweetcorn salad

Salad leaves (e.g. lettuce, rocket, and watercress)

EVENING MEAL

Spicy butter beans with sweet potatoes

Baked apples with fruit and nuts

SNACKS

Celery, carrot and cucumber sticks dipped in a little hummus

Small handful of nuts (e.g. walnuts, almonds, or cashews)

BROWN RICE AND SWEETCORN SALAD

MAKES 2 SERVINGS

175g (6oz) rice
2 spring onions, chopped
1 red pepper, chopped
60g (2oz) sultanas
25g (1oz) flaked toasted almonds
125g (4oz) sweetcorn

Cook the rice according to directions on the packet. Drain if necessary, rinse in cold water and drain again.

Place in a large bowl and combine with the remaining ingredients.

SPICY BUTTER BEANS WITH SWEET POTATOES

MAKES 2 SERVINGS

1 medium sweet potato (weighing about 300g/10oz), peeled and
    diced
1 tablespoon (15ml) extra-virgin olive oil
1 small onion, chopped
1 clove garlic, crushed
1 teaspoon (5ml) medium curry paste (or according to taste)
200g (7oz) tinned chopped tomatoes
40g (1½oz) button mushrooms, halved
200g (7oz) tinned butter beans, drained
1 teaspoon (5ml) each chopped fresh coriander and mint

Cook the sweet potatoes in a steamer or in boiling water for 5 minutes
until they are just soft but firm. Drain.

Heat the olive oil in a large pan. Add the onion and garlic and fry for
5 minutes.

Add the curry paste and cook, stirring continuously for 1 minute.
Add the tomatoes, mushrooms, chickpeas and the sweet potatoes.
Bring to the boil then simmer for 10 minutes.

Just before serving, stir in the chopped fresh herbs. Transfer to a
serving dish.

BAKED APPLES WITH FRUIT AND NUTS

MAKES 2 SERVINGS

2 Bramley cooking apples
1 tablespoon (15ml) raisins or sultanas
6–8 ready-to-eat dried apricots, chopped
2 teaspoons (10ml) clear honey
1 tablespoon (15ml) pecans, chopped

Preheat the oven to 190C/375F/gas mark 5.

Remove the core from the apples. Using a sharp knife, lightly score the skin around the middle, just enough to pierce the skin.

In a small bowl, combine the dried fruit, honey and pecans. Fill the cavities of the apples, then place them in a baking dish. They should fit snugly side by side. Add 2 tablespoons of water, cover loosely with foil then bake for 45 to 60 minutes.

Check a few times during cooking, adding a little extra water if the dish becomes dry.

Serve warm with plain live bio-yoghurt.

BREAKFAST

Porridge with raisins and apricots (see recipe, page 64)

LUNCH

Stir-fried vegetables with cashews

One portion (125g/4oz) fresh fruit

(e.g. 1 banana, 2 kiwi fruit, 2 clementines)

with 1 pot plain soya or bio-yoghurt

EVENING MEAL

Spicy millet with roasted hazelnuts

Poached plums with ginger

SNACKS

1 pot plain soya yoghurt or natural bio-yoghurt mixed with

125g (4oz) fresh fruit (e.g. strawberries, banana or blueberries)

STIR-FRIED VEGETABLES WITH CASHEWS

MAKES 2 SERVINGS

1 tablespoon (15ml) olive or rapeseed oil
1 small onion, sliced
1 teaspoon (5ml) grated fresh ginger
1 garlic clove, crushed
85g (3oz) broccoli florets
85g (3oz) thin green beans, trimmed
1 courgette, sliced
125g (4oz) bean sprouts
1 tablespoon (15ml) water
1 tablespoon (15ml) light soy sauce
60g (2oz) cashew nuts, toasted

Heat the rapeseed oil in a nonstick wok or large frying pan. Add the onion, ginger and garlic and stir-fry for 2 minutes.

Add the broccoli, green beans and courgette and stir-fry for a further 2 to 3 minutes.

Add the bean sprouts, water and soy sauce, and continue stir-frying for a further minute.

Stir in the cashew nuts and serve.

SPICY MILLET WITH ROASTED HAZELNUTS

MAKES 2 SERVINGS

1 tablespoon (15ml) extra-virgin olive oil
1 small onion, chopped
Half a red pepper, deseeded and chopped
Half a teaspoon (2.5ml) cumin
Half a teaspoon (2.5ml) turmeric
125g (4oz) millet
300ml (½ pint) vegetable stock
125g (4oz) frozen peas
40g (1½oz) hazelnuts
Juice of 1 lemon
Small handful chopped fresh mint

Heat the oil in a large heavy-based pan and cook the onion and red pepper for 5 minutes over a moderate heat. Add the spices and fry for 1 minute, stirring continually.

Add the millet and the vegetable stock, bring to the boil, cover and simmer for 20 minutes, stirring occasionally until the stock has been absorbed and the millet is light and fluffy. Add the peas during the last 5 minutes of the cooking time.

Place the hazelnuts in a frying pan over a high heat for 2 to 3 minutes until lightly toasted, shaking the pan occasionally.

Stir the nuts, lemon juice and mint into the millet mixture and serve.

POACHED PLUMS WITH GINGER

MAKES 2 SERVINGS

125ml (4fl oz) water
1 tablespoon (15ml) clear honey
225g (8oz) purple plums
2.5cm (1-inch) piece root ginger, chopped

Place the water and honey in a saucepan and bring slowly to the boil, stirring occasionally until the honey has dissolved.

Halve the plums and remove the stones. Add to the honey liquor with the chopped ginger. Simmer gently for 10 minutes until the plums are tender.

Cover and chill in the fridge until required. Serve the plums and their liquor with plain soya or bio-yoghurt.

BREAKFAST

Plate of fresh fruit – at least 2 portions

e.g. satsumas, pears, grapes, strawberries, bananas

Small pot of soya (150ml/5fl oz) of bio-yoghurt mixed with 1
tablespoon (15ml) toasted nuts (e.g. almonds, cashews) or seeds

LUNCH

Butternut squash soup

Slice of rye (or other non-wheat) bread or 2 rye or rice crackers

One portion (125g/4oz) fresh fruit (e.g. 1 apple, pear or banana)

EVENING MEAL

Red-lentil dhal with sunflower seeds

3 tablespoons (45ml) cooked brown rice

Melon and mango skewers

SNACKS

125g (4oz) fresh fruit (e.g. 2 satsumas or clementines)

Small handful of toasted seeds

(e.g. pumpkin, sunflower or sesame seeds)

BUTTERNUT SQUASH SOUP

MAKES 2 SERVINGS

Half a medium butternut squash
500ml (¾ pint) vegetable stock
1 small onion, chopped
Half a small swede, peeled and chopped
1 tablespoon (15ml) extra-virgin olive oil
A little low-sodium salt and freshly ground black pepper

Peel the butternut squash and cut the flesh into chunks.

Place the vegetable stock, butternut squash, onion and swede in a large saucepan. Bring to the boil, lower the heat, cover and simmer for about 20 minutes until the vegetables are tender.

Remove from the heat and liquidise with the olive oil until smooth using a blender, food processor or a hand blender.

Return to the saucepan to heat through. Season the soup with the low-sodium salt and freshly ground black pepper.

RED-LENTIL DHAL WITH SUNFLOWER SEEDS

MAKES 2 SERVINGS

1 onion, chopped
1 tablespoon (15ml) water or vegetable stock
1–2 garlic cloves, crushed
Half a teaspoon (2.5ml) ground cumin
1 teaspoon (5ml) ground coriander
Half a teaspoon (2.5ml) turmeric
175g (6oz) red lentils
600ml (1 pint) water
60g (2oz) sunflower seeds
1 tablespoon (15ml) olive oil
Low-sodium salt to season
Handful of fresh coriander or parsley, finely chopped

Sauté the onion in the water or stock for a few minutes. Add the garlic and spices and cook for one more minute.

Add the lentils and water and bring to the boil. Cover and simmer for about 20 minutes. Alternatively, cook in a pressure cooker for 3 minutes then turn off the heat.

Stir in the sunflower seeds, olive oil, salt and fresh coriander or parsley.

MELON AND MANGO SKEWERS

MAKES 2 SERVINGS

2 apricots
Half a cantaloupe melon
1 nectarine
1 small mango, peeled and stoned

Halve the apricots and remove the stones. Cut the melon in half and scoop out the seeds. Either scoop out the flesh using a melon baler, or slice then cut into cubes. Slice the nectarine and cut the mango flesh into chunks.

Thread the fruit onto 4 wooden skewers, making sure that each has a mixture of fruit. Serve immediately.

INDEX